LIVING ON MARS
CAN YOU COLONIZE A PLANET

David Hawksett

PowerKiDS press.

New York

$$d = \sqrt{(x_2 - x_1) + (y_2 - y_1)^2}$$

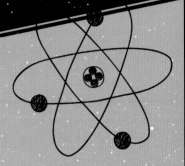

Published in 2018 by **The Rosen Publishing Group, Inc.**
29 East 21st Street, New York, NY 10010

Cataloging-in-Publication Data
Names: Hawksett, David.
Title: Living on Mars: can you colonize a planet? / David Hawksett.
Description: New York : PowerKids Press, 2018. | Series: Be a space scientist! | Includes index.
Identifiers: ISBN 9781538322987 (pbk.) | ISBN 9781538322055 (library bound) | ISBN 9781538322994 (6 pack)
Subjects: LCSH: Space flight to Mars--Juvenile literature. | Space colonies--Juvenile literature. | Mars (Planet)--
    Exploration--Juvenile literature.
Classification: LCC TL799.M3 H39 2018 | DDC 523.43--dc23

Produced for Rosen by Calcium
Editors for Calcium: Sarah Eason and Jennifer Sanderson
Designers for Calcium: Paul Myerscough and Jeni Child
Picture Researcher: Rachel Blount

Photo Credits: Cover: NASA: Image courtesy: European Space Agency fg, Shutterstock: Vadim Sadovski bg; Inside:
NASA: NASA Earth Observatory images by Robert Simmon, using Suomi NPP VIIRS data from Chris Elvidge (NOAA
National Geophysical Data Center) 9tl, NASA Goddard Space Flight Center 8bl, NASA/Goddard/Lunar Reconnaissance
Orbiter 9cl, NASA/JHU Applied Physics Lab/Carnegie Inst. Washington 8cl, NASA/JPL-Caltech/MSSS 9bl; Shutterstock:
AuntSpray 5b, 10, Everett Historical 6bl, Harvepino 4–5, Monkey Business Images 33, Muratart 6–7, Vadim Sadovski
28, Alfonso de Tomas 14–15; Wikimedia Commons: Neil Armstrong/NASA 21, Daein Ballard 42–43b, Creative Tools
40l, Charlie Duke/NASA 12–13, D Ramey Logan 23b, NASA 11, 19t, 22–23, 29, 30l, 32, 34b, 38, 39, NASA Ames
Research Center 43t, NASA Goddard Space Flight Center 20, NASA/JPL 16–17, NASA/JPL-Caltech/Corby Waste 26–
27, NASA/JPL-Caltech/Cornell Univ./Arizona State Univ 18–19, NASA/JPL/MSSS 37c, NASA/JPL-Caltech/University of
Arizona 17b, NASA/JPL-Caltech/USGS 1, 27c, 36–37, NASA/Paolo Nespoli 24, Rlevente 34–35, SpaceX Photos 25,
30–31.

Manufactured in China
CPSIA Compliance Information: Batch BW18PK: For Further Information contact Rosen Publishing, New York, New York at 1-800-237-9932.

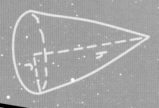

CONTENTS

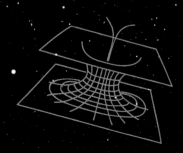

Chapter 1
A SECOND HOME IN SPACE?

Earth is our home planet. It formed from the dust in the **solar nebula** around 4.5 billion years ago. Although life on Earth began as **microbes** very quickly after the birth of our planet, human beings did not appear until three million years ago. Like all other **organisms** on Earth, humans have **evolved** to suit Earth's **environment**. Our eyes are **adapted** to see in full sunlight. Our lungs work perfectly with Earth's **atmosphere** at sea level, and our skeletons are designed to cope with Earth's **gravity**.

Our Dangerous World

Although Earth is the only place we know of that has life, it is also a dangerous place. Just think of the **extinction** of the dinosaurs 65 million years ago. We know an **asteroid** around 6.2 miles (10 km) wide hit Earth at this time, and massive volcanic eruptions also affected Earth's **climate**. The asteroid punched a hole in Earth's surface 112 miles (180 km) wide, but this crater was discovered only in the 1990s. It was not just the dinosaurs that suffered — around three-quarters of all plant and animal **species** became extinct.

Going back even further, around 252 million years ago, another **mass extinction** took place. It is known as "The Great Dying." Nobody is sure whether volcanic activity, an asteroid, or something else caused it, but an incredible 96% of all species on Earth were wiped out.

A Home on Mars?

Earth is still not safe today! Volcanoes and asteroids threaten us. We also face new disasters that are more likely to be caused by humans than nature. **Climate change**, **overpopulation**, pollution, and **nuclear disasters** are just some of the problems humans have created. Earth is our home, but it is under threat. One day, people may need a new place to live. If we are to make sure that the human race survives, we need a second home in space. That home may be on Mars.

$$d = \sqrt{(x_2 - x_1) + (y_2 - y_1)^2}$$

The explosion that made the world's dinosaurs extinct was more than a billion times greater than the atomic bombs dropped on Hiroshima and Nagasaki during World War II.

THE HISTORY OF MARS

Ancient **civilizations** were fascinated by special stars that moved slowly across the sky over days, weeks, and months. The ancient Greeks named them *planetes*, meaning "wanderer." The five planets that you can see with the naked eye (without a **telescope**) were named for their gods. The Greeks named them Hermes, Aphrodite, Ares, Zeus, and Cronus. However, we are more familiar with their Roman names: Mercury, Venus, Mars, Jupiter, and Saturn.

Looking for Life

Although Mars is not the brightest of the planets in the night sky, it stands out because of its color. On a clear night, Mars appears as a bright star, but its orangey-red color led the ancient Greeks and Romans to name it after their god of war, because it was the color of blood. It is also called the "red planet" due to its color.

Italian astronomer Galileo Galilei (1564–1642) was the first person to look at Mars through a telescope, although the telescope's low power meant that he could not see any detail. As telescopes became bigger and more powerful, bright and dark patches on Mars's surface were seen, including bright white **polar caps**. It was then that astronomers noticed that Mars was similar to Earth in many ways.

The telescope was invented in 1608, but Galileo first used it for astronomy in 1609. He studied the moon and discovered Jupiter's moons.

$$d = \sqrt{(x_2 - x_1)}$$

Mars

canyon

In the late 1800s, another Italian astronomer, Giovanni Schiaparelli (1835–1910), claimed to see long, dark lines on Mars through his telescope. People started to believe these lines were canals, dug by aliens living on Mars. They believed the aliens used the canals to bring water from the polar caps! We now know that the lines were an **optical illusion**.

Learning More About Mars

It was not until the **Space Age** that people were able to see Mars close up, from space **probes** and **landers**. While much of the planet is covered with craters, other parts contain some of the greatest wonders of the **solar system**. The first probe to **orbit** Mars was *Mariner 9*. It journeyed to Mars in 1971 and discovered giant volcanoes, such as Olympus Mons, that are much bigger than any on Earth. Olympus Mons rises to a height of nearly 13.6 miles (22 km), which is around 2.5 times the height of Mount Everest. *Mariner 9* also discovered a canyon more than 2,500 miles (4,023 km) long and up to 23,000 feet (7,000 m) deep.

WHY COLONIZE MARS?

With the exception of the sun, if we look at the bodies of the inner solar system (Mercury, Venus, Earth, the moon, and Mars), each world has its own properties. Some of these are listed below. Look at some of the numbers and compare them to Earth's. Then imagine what it would be like for an astronaut on the surface of each body. For example, on the moon, there is no atmosphere, so you would need a spacesuit to survive there. However, its low gravity means that you could jump six times higher than on Earth. The more different a planet is from Earth, the harder it would be to survive there.

The Bodies of Our Inner Solar System

Mercury
Diameter: 3,302 miles (5,314 km)
Gravity (Earth = 1): 0.38
Length of day (24 hours = 1 day): 58.6 days
Temperature: -274 °F to 842 °F (-170 °C to 450 °C)
Atmosphere: None

Venus
Diameter: 7,521 miles (12,104 km)
Gravity (Earth = 1): 0.9
Length of day (24 hours = 1 day): 243 days
Temperature: 869 °F (465 °C)
Atmosphere: Almost all carbon dioxide (almost 100 times thicker than Earth's)

Earth
Diameter: 7,926 miles (12,756 km)
Gravity (Earth = 1): 1
Length of day (24 hours = 1 day): 1
Temperature: -128° F to 136° F
Atmosphere: Nitrogen, oxygen, and carbon dioxide

Moon
Diameter: 2,159 miles (3,475 km)
Gravity (Earth = 1): 0.16
Length of day (24 hours = 1 day): 29 days
Temperature: -279 °F to 261 °F (-88 °C to 58 °C)
Atmosphere: None

Mars
Diameter: 4,221 miles (6,793 km)
Gravity (Earth = 1): 0.38
Length of day (24 hours = 1 day): 1 day 7 hours
Temperature: -193 °F to 68 °F (-125 °C to 20 °C)
Atmosphere: Carbon dioxide (100 times thinner than Earth's)

Be a Space Scientist!

1. Find the body that has the gravity most similar to Earth's. This place would be the easiest world to walk on because our sense of balance is suited to Earth's gravity. Does this world have any other qualities that make it a great or a terrible place to live?

2. Aside from Earth, which place has the best temperature for humans to survive? What other feature does this world have that makes it similar to Earth?

3. When you compare the surface qualities of all the inner solar system worlds, why do you think that space agencies feel Mars is the best choice of planet to colonize in the future?

Chapter 2
HUMANS TO THE MOON

Colonizing Mars started in the 1960s with the first missions to the moon. These were the very first human journeys into space, and they paved the way for future missions to planets such as Mars.

Racing into Space

In the 1960s, the United States and the Union of Soviet Socialist Republics (USSR) were deep into the **Cold War**. The Cold War got this name because neither side actually fought the other. Instead, both built **missiles** that could carry a **nuclear bomb** across continents. Many of the scientists that developed these missiles wanted to use them to send probes into space. Both the United States and the USSR began doing this as a way to show the world its technical abilities. The competition between them became known as the "Space Race."

In 1957, the USSR won the first space race, which was to launch a **satellite** into space. *Sputnik 1* did not do much more than send out beeps, but the world was still impressed. When the USSR sent Yuri Gagarin (1934–1938) into space in 1961, the world was even more impressed. He was the first man in space! The attention made the United States aim for the most impressive goal of them all: landing on the Moon.

Sputnik 1 *was a metal sphere just under 2 feet (0.6 m) across. The spikes you can see are its radio transmitters.*

$$d = \sqrt{(x_2 - x_1) + (y_2}$$

Race for the Moon

US President John F. Kennedy made an important speech in 1962. In it, he committed the United States to sending people to the moon, and of course, returning them safely to Earth. To find out more about the moon, robot scouts called Ranger probes were sent there. Their job was to find a safe place to land and take photographs of the moon's surface. Each probe was fired at the moon like a bullet. When it hit the moon's surface, it smashed into pieces. Before it hit the moon, it took photographs of it and beamed them back to Earth. The United States also sent the *Lunar Orbiter* probes into space to orbit the moon and send thousands of images back home.
Then came the *Surveyor* missions, which were landers designed to survive for a short time on the surface of the moon and record what its conditions were like.

All these missions paved the way for humans by finding safe landing sites. Finally, in 1969, the United States was ready to send *Apollo 11* to the moon. This was to be the first mission in which humans landed on the moon.

Ranger 4 launched on April 23, 1962, on top of an Atlas rocket. It crashed on the far side of the moon without beaming back any images, but it was the first US probe to touch another world.

11

LIVING ON THE MOON

Apollo 11 successfully landed on the moon on July 20, 1969. After that, six more Apollo missions followed. Each mission was longer and more complicated than the previous one. *Apollo 13* almost ended in total disaster when an oxygen tank exploded on the spacecraft. The others all landed safely in the lunar module.

$$d = \sqrt{(x_2 - x_1) + (y_2 - y_1)^2}$$

The Lunar Module

The lunar module was the only manned spacecraft ever built that was not meant to cope with launching or landing in an atmosphere. As a result, it was spindly and fragile but also extremely light. To land, a light spacecraft needs a small, reliable engine. If the spacecraft is damaged while landing, it may not be able to take off again, and the astronauts would be stranded on the moon with no hope of rescue. The lunar module had to be a safe home for the astronauts to return to, just like a spacecraft. Inside, it was very cramped. However, there was just enough room for the two astronauts to sleep and put on and remove their spacesuits.

A Tough Place to Be

The 12 astronauts who landed on the moon during the Apollo missions found the lack of gravity comfortable, but out on the surface, the conditions were harsh. The lack of air on the moon makes temperatures much more extreme than on Earth, even though Earth and the moon are the same distance from the sun. In full sunlight, the moon can reach 261 °F (127 °C), while in the shade, it drops instantly to a temperature of -279 °F (-173 °C).

Neil Armstrong (1930–2012) and Buzz Aldrin (b. 1930) spent just 21.5 hours on the Moon during *Apollo 11*'s mission. They left the lander once and spent 2.5 hours walking on the surface. They collected rock and dust samples and planted the US flag. By the time of *Apollo 17* in 1972, the last mission, the astronauts had much more work to do. This time, the two astronauts, Gene Cernan (1934–2017) and Harrison Schmitt (b. 1935), performed three moonwalks and spent just over three days living on the moon.

John Young leaps off the ground as he salutes during Apollo 16. You can see the moon buggy parked in front of the lunar module. John went to the moon twice and flew the space shuttle.

GETTING DRESSED FOR SPACE

$$d = \sqrt{(x_2 - x_1) + (y_2 - y_1)^2}$$

Space is a dangerous place for humans to be. To help them stay safe, astronauts wear spacesuits. Astronauts use spacesuits today when they perform spacewalks outside the International Space Station (ISS) to install new equipment or make repairs.

Suited for Walking in Space

The first person to ever walk in space was **cosmonaut** Alexey Leonov (b. 1934) in 1965. His walk lasted just 12 minutes and nearly ended in tragedy. Like all spacesuits, Alexey's had to contain a miniature version of Earth's atmosphere so that he could breathe. However, in space, his suit behaved like a **pressurized** balloon. It expanded, and Alexey could not fit back inside the spacecraft. He made a risky decision and opened a valve on his suit, allowing some of his air to rush into space. Alexey was only able to get back inside after he deflated his suit to below safe levels.

Apollo Suits

The Apollo suit for walking on the moon was much more advanced. It was designed to be dustproof so that fine lunar dust did not clog up any joints or seals on the spacecraft. It had a cooling system to keep the astronaut from overheating. Water was pumped around in tubes inside the suit. It also included a life-support backpack, which kept the astronaut supplied with oxygen and removed the harmful carbon dioxide he breathed out. The spacesuit weighed 180 pounds (82 kg), which is around the same weight as fully grown man. Spacesuits used for spacewalks on the space shuttle were heavier, about 310 pounds (141 kg).

helmet with visor

V camera

gloves

Manned Maneuvering Unit with thrusters that allow spacewalks without a **tether**

spacesuit with cooling and life support

Be a Space Scientist!

Look at the information about Mars and the Moon on page 9. What do you notice when you compare the gravity of both bodies? Using this information, what do you think will need to be different about a Mars spacesuit, and why?

Chapter 3
PAVING THE WAY TO MARS

Since the mid-1960s, dozens of robots called probes have been sent to Mars to find out more about the planet. Most probes were sent by the United States and the USSR, but more recently, Europe and India have sent their own successful missions.

Failed Missions

The story of **robotic** Mars exploration has been full of difficulties. More than half of the missions have failed. Some blew up while launching from Earth. Some crashed into Mars instead of landing gently. One even crashed into Mars because of a mathematical error. Some lost contact with Earth, leading some scientists to joke about a "Great Galactic Ghoul" that likes to eat Mars probes.

This is a Viking image of Olympus Mons. The craters at the top were not formed by impacts but by explosive volcanic eruptions that took place millions of years ago. White clouds surround the base of the volcano.

Mission Successful!

The first probe to orbit Mars was *Mariner 9* in 1971. Within a month, the USSR's *Mars 2* and *Mars 3* were also successful. When *Mariner 9* arrived, Mars was completely covered in a global dust storm that lasted for months. Finally, the dust settled, and the probe was able to photograph Mars's great volcanoes and its gigantic Mariner Valley.

Four years later, the National Aeronautics and Space Administration's (NASA's) Viking probes arrived. These were two identical spacecraft, which were designed to spend several years orbiting and collecting information from the planet. They also both carried a lander with them. These landers made the first successful touchdowns on Mars.

Send in the Robots

Since Viking, there have been more Mars orbiters. Some have been successful while others failed. By 2017, there were a total of six working spacecraft orbiting Mars and two **rovers** on its surface. Mars orbiters study the surface from space and also act as communications satellites for each other. However, there is only so much you can learn about a planet from space. To find out what it is really like, you need to send robot landers to the surface.

The Viking landers were loaded with scientific instruments. The robot arm with the soil sampler is in the foreground. The dish on the top beams its findings back to Earth.

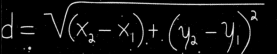

$$d = \sqrt{(x_2 - x_1) + (y_2 - y_1)}^2$$

LANDERS ON MARS

$$d = \sqrt{(x_2 - x_1) + (y_2 - y_1)^2}$$

In 1971, the USSR sent *Mars 2* and *Mars 3* to land on Mars. *Mars 2* became the first human-made object to touch the planet's surface. It was destroyed when its parachute failed to open, but *Mars 3* touched down gently. A **heat shield** was used to slow it down, changing the energy of the probe's speed into heat. Parachutes, then **retro-rockets**, slowed the probe before landing.

The Great Galactic Ghoul Strikes Again

Mars 3 began its work right away, but just 14.5 seconds after landing, communications with Earth became silent. The probe managed to send one part of a picture to Earth, but nothing can be seen in it. The Great Galactic Ghoul had claimed another victim!

The Viking Missions

It was NASA's Viking landers that achieved the goal of landing and working properly on Mars's surface. Like *Mars 3*, they used heat shields to slow them down from orbit. A parachute then opened when the landers had slowed enough not to tear it. Finally, rockets fired at the last second for a gentle landing. *Viking 1* lasted 1 year, 11 months on Mars, while *Viking 2* lasted 3 years, 7 months on Mars. They carried scientific instruments to measure weather patterns and tools to collect samples of the Martian soil. They also looked for signs of microbes in the soil.

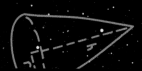

Roving Across Mars

In 1997, the first lander with a rover went to Mars. *Sojourner* was the size of a microwave oven. It took pictures and studied the **chemistry** of the rocks. *Spirit* and *Opportunity* were larger and more advanced than *Sojourner*. *Opportunity* is still going strong after landing in 2004 and traveling more than 27 miles (43.5 km) across Mars. The latest rover, *Curiosity*, is the size of a car. Since 2012, it has been roving the planet, looking for signs of ancient life.

Sojourner *spent three months studying the rocks near the landing site. The flat top is a solar panel to generate electricity from sunlight for the rover to use.*

A camera on top of the mast of the Opportunity *rover looks down and takes a "selfie." You can see how dusty its solar panels have become!*

CHOOSING WHERE TO LAND

Imagine exploring Earth from space for the first time. At first, you would realize that some parts are blue, and others are green or brown. You would notice that there are white parts at the top and bottom of the planet. How would decide where to land for the first time? If you tried to land on the blue area, you would be in trouble if your spacecraft could not float. You would also need to make sure you did not land on an active volcano — but you would need to study Earth from space for a long time before you even knew that the planet has volcanoes! A crew trying to land on Mars would face just as many hazards.

Even though the air on Mars is thin, dust storms often happen. The dust is fine in size, and the low gravity helps the storms form. In December 2015, lightning was detected in Martian dust storms for the first time.

Landing Dangers

No human has yet landed on Mars, but we know a lot about the dangers of landing a vehicle on another planet from the missions to the moon. When *Apollo 11* became the first manned mission to land on the moon, the landing site had been chosen in advance using the knowledge gathered by the Surveyor, Orbiter, and Ranger missions. However, as *Apollo 11* approached this landing site, Neil Armstrong looked out the window and saw that it was covered in huge boulders, which would have wrecked the spacecraft. Fortunately, he found a smoother location to land the craft.

Be a Space Scientist!

Imagine the dangers you would face landing a human crew on Mars. How do you think the storms on Mars would affect a crew attempting to land there? Why?

The lunar module is the top half of this spacecraft. It has its own engine, which leaves the bottom half behind when it blasts off. The bottom half with the legs had a separate engine for the landing.

Apollo 11 was much heavier than the robot scouts, so some scientists were afraid that the lunar module lander would simply sink deep beneath the lunar dust. When Armstrong and Aldrin climbed down the ladder to walk on the moon, the last step was so big that they had to jump to get back up. The legs of the lunar module were made longer in case the lander started to sink. Fortunately, it did not sink. But this situation shows how careful you must be during the exploration of a new place.

$$d = \sqrt{(x_a - x_i)^2 + (y_a - y_i)^2}$$

Chapter 4
THE RACE TO MARS

Sputnik 1, launched in 1957 by the USSR, was Earth's first human-made satellite. Its launch marked the start of the Space Age, a time in history when space exploration became possible. The launch of *Sputnik 1* achieved many firsts for the USSR. The first human, Yuri Gagarin, was sent into space. With him went the first space crew, who also established the first **space station**.

The Cost of Space Travel

The Space Age has achieved many great things so far, but space travel has not been cheap. In 1962, when President Kennedy promised that the United States would be first to land people on the moon, he called it the "most hazardous and dangerous and greatest adventure on which man has ever embarked." He did not say how much it would cost. The Apollo Program, which sent six missions to the moon, cost $25 billion. In today's money, that is more than $100 billion.

This is the first flight of the space shuttle.
Columbia launched on April 12, 1981, piloted by
Apollo astronauts John Young and Robert Crippen.
Their mission lasted two days and six hours.

$$d = \sqrt{(x_2 - x_1) + (y_2 - y_1)}$$

The Space Shuttle

The United States's next big space project was the space shuttle. The space shuttle took off like a rocket but landed like a glider. Unlike previous space launchers, the shuttle was built to be reused. From the first flight of *Columbia* in 1981 to the final flight of *Atlantis* in 2011, NASA flew 133 successful shuttle missions. However, not all the missions were successful. Two shuttles exploded, and both crews died. The space shuttle was eventually canceled because of its cost and safety record. It was supposed to be much cheaper than the rockets it replaced, but it was not. By the end of its service, it had cost around $450 million for each launch.

A New Kind of Space Race

Until 2003, only the United States and Russia had sent people into space. Then China joined the club when Chinese astronaut Yang Liwei (b. 1965) completed his first mission. The following year, the company Scaled Composites sent an astronaut just beyond the edge of space in a spaceplane named *SpaceShipOne*. That spacecraft is now owned by Richard Branson's Virgin Galactic company, which will soon send people into space just for fun. Since 2004, others have started designing and launching rockets into space. These include Jeff Bezos, the owner of Amazon, and Elon Musk, who made his money from his company, PayPal. It looks certain that billionaires, rather than governments, will win the new Space Race.

SpaceShipOne became the first manned spaceflight that was not paid for by a government. It launched from underneath an aircraft at high altitude and landed like a glider.

N328KF

INTERNATIONAL MISSION

During the Cold War and the Space Race, the United States and the USSR saw each other as rivals. However, many of the scientists on both sides wanted to work with each other. After the last Apollo mission to the moon in 1972, the United States and the USSR worked together on Apollo-Soyuz. In July 1975, each country sent a crew in a space capsule into orbit around Earth. There, the capsules docked and the crews met. The moment they opened the hatch and shook hands marked the first major international event in space.

The ISS is around the size of a football field. You can see its solar panels, which provide power. You can also see the space shuttle Endeavour docked at the top.

The ISS

In 1998, astronauts began working on the ISS. The project plan was so expensive that no single country wanted to pay for it. Now that the ISS is complete, it carries the flags of the 26 countries that helped build it. It has cost more than $150 billion so far. The money comes from governments that also pay for education, defense, and health care.

Many people complain that the ISS is a waste of government money. However, now that billionaires like Elon Musk (see page 23) are building their own rockets, less money will be needed from governments to fund space travel.

Vacations in Space?

Space tourism began in 2001, when US millionaire Denis Tito paid around $20 million to visit the ISS. Six more people have followed, with the money from their tickets helping to fund the ISS. Elon Musk's company, SpaceX, has already launched its own rockets into space. The company has even landed rockets on Earth safely, so that they can be used again for other trips into space. In 2012, SpaceX sent an unmanned capsule, filled with supplies, to the ISS. It was the first private company to do so. Musk plans to send humans to Mars, but like Apollo, this will be very expensive. When it does happen, hopefully within the next 20 years, the astronauts will probably have the flags of many countries and many private companies on their spacesuits.

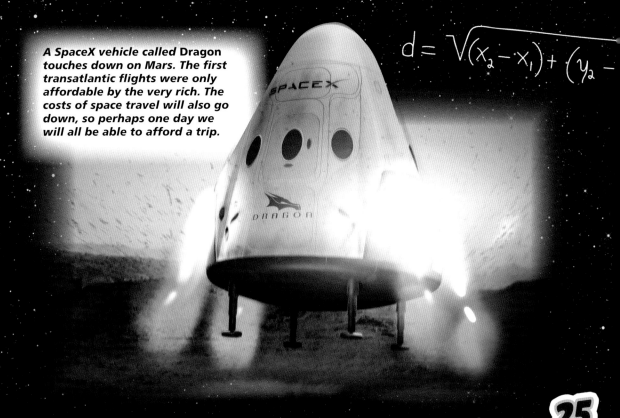

A SpaceX vehicle called Dragon touches down on Mars. The first transatlantic flights were only affordable by the very rich. The costs of space travel will also go down, so perhaps one day we will all be able to afford a trip.

SETTING UP BASE

$$d = \sqrt{(x_2 - x_1) +}$$

We have seen already that if you want to send people to another world, you need to know exactly where you plan to land. You could not send people to Mars and then hope they would find a good spot by looking out of the window.

Planning Ahead

From the many flybys, orbiters, and landers, we now know a lot about Mars. We can see what it looks like from space, and we have seen what it is like on the ground. That knowledge can be used to plan where to build a Mars base that people could live in.

Mapping Mars

There are now many different maps of Mars, made from pictures taken by spacecraft. We are most familiar with maps that show the shape of the land. These are called **topographic maps**. There are others that show the warmest and coldest places, using **infrared**. Some maps show where rocks and **minerals** can be found.

The Mars Global Surveyor reached Mars in September 1997. It spent nine years orbiting the planet. One of its most exciting discoveries was that liquid water seemed to seep from the ground in some craters.

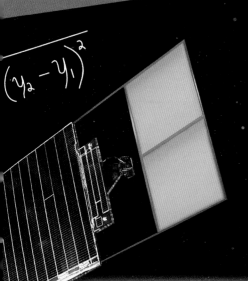

Using MOLA

The topographic map (shown below) was made using a scientific instrument called MOLA onboard the *Mars Global Surveyor* spacecraft. MOLA stands for Mars Orbiter Laser Altimeter. MOLA used a narrow beam of light, or laser, to measure the heights of all the features on Mars. The heights are shown by color. The highest parts are red, and the lowest are blue, with shades of orange, yellow, and green in between. Like on Earth, the atmosphere on Mars is thickest at low points and thinnest on mountaintops. Thicker air contains more oxygen, which humans need to breathe. The temperatures are also warmest nearer the equator, which runs through the middle of the map. If Mars had oceans, they would fill the blue areas. You can even see the giant volcanoes on the left of the map.

The MOLA map shows that the northern half of Mars is much flatter and lower than the southern half. The blue circle is a crater named Hellas.

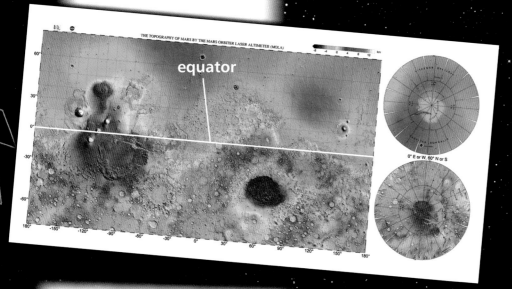

THE TOPOGRAPHY OF MARS BY THE MARS ORBITER LASER ALTIMETER (MOLA)

equator

0° E or W, 60° N or S

Be a Space Scientist!

Imagine you are in charge of where to build a Mars base. What decisions will you make using the topographic map above? Give reasons for your answer.

Chapter 5
HUMANS TO MARS

Apart from Earth, the moon is the only other place people have been to in the solar system. It is Earth's natural satellite, and it is nearby compared to Mars and the other planets. The moon is 238,900 miles (384,472 km) away.

Changing Distance

The distance between Earth and Mars changes because both planets orbit the sun at different speeds, with Mars farther out and slower. When Earth and Mars are both on the same side as the sun, the distance between them is around 40 million miles (64 million km). That is nearly 170 times farther away than the moon. However, when Earth and Mars are on opposite sides of the sun, the distance can be as great as 250 million miles (402 million km), which is more than 1,000 times farther away than the moon!

$$d = \sqrt{(x_2 - x_1) + (y_2 - y_1)^2}$$

Teams of engineers and scientists monitor missions from the ground. This is mission control in Houston, Texas. From here, NASA controls manned space missions.

Why Distance Matters

In space, distances affect communication. Radio signals travel at the speed of light, which is 186,282 miles per second (299,792 km/s). Even at this speed, it takes radio signals under 1.5 seconds to reach the Moon. You can hear this in the recordings of Apollo missions. When **mission control** spoke to the astronauts, there was a pause for a few seconds before they got a reply. When Mars and Earth are closest together, it would take 3.5 minutes for a radio signal to travel from one planet to another. This means that astronauts on Mars would not be able to talk to Earth in a normal conversation. It would take 7 minutes to receive an answer to a question. The distance between Earth and Mars also means that the journey would take much longer than the 3 days it took for the Apollo missions to reach the moon. Reaching Mars could take more than 200 days.

A SPECIAL SPACECRAFT

The spacecraft used to reach Mars would need to be a lot more advanced that the one used to reach the moon. A manned mission to Mars will need a spacecraft that can keep the crew alive for around 200 days, the time it would take to get to Mars. The spacecraft would also need to be bigger than the Apollo capsules, which needed to carry only around one week's worth of oxygen, food, and water. The spacecraft will need a massive rocket to get it off the ground.

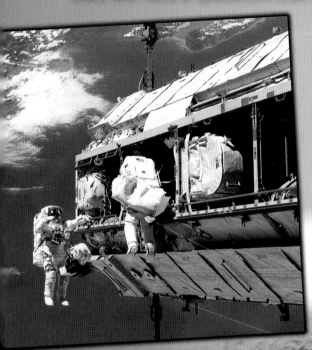

Astronauts often perform spacewalks on the outside of the ISS. They make repairs and add components to it. A Mars spacecraft could be built in orbit or even while docked to the Space Station.

Launching the Spacecraft

It is quite possible that the Mars ship will be too large to be launched from Earth by one rocket, and it may take several launches to send its parts into orbit. Astronauts have been building and modifying the ISS for almost 20 years, which is great practice for assembling a Mars ship in orbit. The Mars ship's parts could even be sent to the ISS to be built there.

More than One Journey

One of the most expensive parts of spaceflight is making a spacecraft safe for people. It is likely that living quarters and other equipment will be sent to Mars beforehand using unmanned rockets. This equipment could land on Mars using the same pinpoint accuracy as previous robot missions. The only people who have died during space exploration are those killed at launch or landing. Sending heavy equipment ahead of the astronauts means that the landing vehicle can be lighter, with a simpler and safer landing. However, it also means that the astronauts would have to land very near the equipment already on the surface so that they could set up their new home.

A SpaceX unmanned capsule is practicing hovering using its rocket engines. The ability to adjust the performance of the spacecraft will be critical in getting people to Mars.

$$d = \sqrt{(x_2 - x_1) + (y_2 - y_1)^2}$$

CHOOSE YOUR CREW

When the United States and the USSR began planning the first manned space missions, they had to decide what kind of people would make the best astronauts. At first, they thought that circus performers would be ideal, because their head for heights and sense of balance would allow them to work in zero gravity without getting sick.

Dr. Harrison Schmitt's expertise was the **geology** of Norway. He spent a whole year learning to fly jets in order to be an astronaut. He worked on the science for all the moon landings, and also helped study the rock and soil samples brought back.

SCHMITT

$$d = \sqrt{(x_2 - x_1)} + (y_2 - y_1)^2$$

On a mission to Mars, the crew will need to be experts in more than one subject. That way, if there is a disaster and some crew members are killed, other members will be able to take on their duties.

The First Space Travelers

The first astronauts and cosmonauts were not from the circus. They were military pilots. Many of them were test pilots, who were some of the bravest and most experienced of all pilots. Test pilots would try out brand-new plane designs without knowing if they would work safely or if they would return to land. For these pilots, flying to space was no more risky. Today's astronauts come from a wider range of occupations. Astronomers, engineers, medical doctors, and people from all sciences now go into space.

More than Pilots

Flying and landing are just part of an astronaut's job. When astronauts explored the moon, they had training in geology so that they could decide on the best rock samples to bring home. During the last Apollo missions, Dr. Harrison Schmitt was on board. Schmitt was a geologist who had trained other astronauts before he was selected himself to join *Apollo 17*. Schmitt had to become a pilot, too, so that he could fly as well as any astronaut.

Be a Space Scientist!

On the ISS, you can leave for Earth quickly if you become seriously sick, but this is impossible on a Mars mission. Instead, you will need to take a doctor who can operate on you in an emergency. Imagine choosing a crew of just six people. In addition to the doctor, what other skills would your crew need? What skills would people need that are similar to those needed for the missions to the moon? Also consider skills that might be needed because Mars is different from the moon and much farther away from Earth.

When *Pathfinder* arrived on Mars in 1997, it was traveling at 4.5 miles per second (7 km/s). To slow down, the spacecraft could have used rockets. However, the extra weight of the engines and the fuel needed to slow down would have made the mission much more expensive.

Slowing Down

Pathfinder used the planet's thin atmosphere to slow down. Hitting the thin Martian air at such high speeds can create enough **friction** to heat up a spacecraft to its destruction. So a heat shield protected the spacecraft from the heat, while the friction slowed it down to a low enough speed for a parachute to open.

As it approached landing, giant airbags inflated around the lander. The lander then separated from the parachute. The airbags made the lander bounce across the surface until it came to a halt. When the lander stopped, the airbags deflated. *Pathfinder* landed gently and in one piece. The *Spirit* and *Opportunity* rovers, which landed in 2004, also used airbags.

Pathfinder relied on its giant airbags to protect it during landing. The airbags softened the impact as the spacecraft made contact with Mars.

$$d = \sqrt{(x_2 - x_1) + \left(y_2 - y_1\right)^2}$$

Landing Equipment

The *Curiosity* rover, which landed on Mars in 2012, was much bigger and too heavy for airbags to be reliable. Instead, it used a sky crane. *Curiosity* entered the Martian atmosphere using a heat shield and a parachute, like the other rovers. Then it detached from the parachute and fired up landing rockets. At the same time, the rover was lowered on a tether underneath the rest of the lander. When the rover's wheels hit the ground, the tether was cut. The rest of the lander flew off to crash a short distance away, so as not to damage the rover itself.

A manned mission will probably use a heat shield, parachute, and landing rockets. In 2015, when SpaceX launched a rocket into space, it landed it back on the ground using its own engines.

The joint European-Russian Schiaparelli lander entered the Martian atmosphere on October 19, 2016. Contact was lost just one minute before landing.

A few days later, NASA took a picture from space using the Mars Reconnaissance Orbiter, which showed that the lander had been destroyed on impact.

LOOKING FOR WATER

Mars's similarity to Earth is what makes us want to go there. Once our mission has landed and our base is set up, the astronauts will have to find water. Without water, they could not survive. Any food they could grow would also need water to survive. Even before probes visited Mars, scientists knew it was likely that there was water or ice on the red planet. The bright white patches at its north and south poles visible through a telescope looked just like our icy polar caps on Earth.

Clues from Orbit

Today, the atmosphere on Mars is way too thin for water to exist as a liquid on the surface. Even at low temperatures, any water would boil off in the Martian air. However, pictures taken by probes in orbit show some curious features. Long, narrow valley networks that look just like river valleys on Earth snake across the Martian landscape. It seems Mars used to have a thicker atmosphere billions of years ago, when water could exist as a liquid.

We know now that the Martian polar caps are mostly water ice. It is likely that ice lies beneath the ground in some areas. More recent probes have even shown water ice filling an old impact crater. An impact crater is a hole made by an asteroid or **comet** strike. Some craters even show dark streaks that change over time, as if ice was melting and running down the crater walls, before bubbling away into the air.

crater

Water from Ice

Our astronauts on Mars will need to find ice close to their base so that they can melt it for drinking and growing food. The *Curiosity* rover is exploring a crater that appears to have once been a shallow sea. This will help our astronauts find water on Mars.

This is Mars's south pole. The white material is ice — mostly water, but with some carbon dioxide.

valley

$$d = \sqrt{(x_2 - x_1) + (y_2 - y_1)^2}$$

SURVIVING MARS

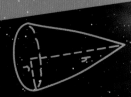

If you spend billions of dollars and 200 days traveling to Mars, it makes sense to stay for longer than a few days. The heavy equipment sent in advance includes a place for astronauts to live in, a laboratory for science experiments, a power source that could be nuclear or solar (from the sun), and the equipment to become self-sufficient. If we could provide water, food, and air on Mars, then we would not need to keep sending supply ships from Earth to the new colony.

Use Your Own

The Martian soil is **sterile**, so to grow vegetables, you would need to add **fertilizers**. Once you start growing plants, you can begin to recycle your air. Plants breathe in carbon dioxide and breathe out oxygen, which is the other way around to humans. People on Mars could also make their own fertilizer for the soil from their own excreted waste. Urine and feces would work well.

To grow fruit, vegetables, and other plants on Mars, you would need to protect them from the cold, thin Martian air. A greenhouse would let in the sunlight but keep the inside at the right temperature.

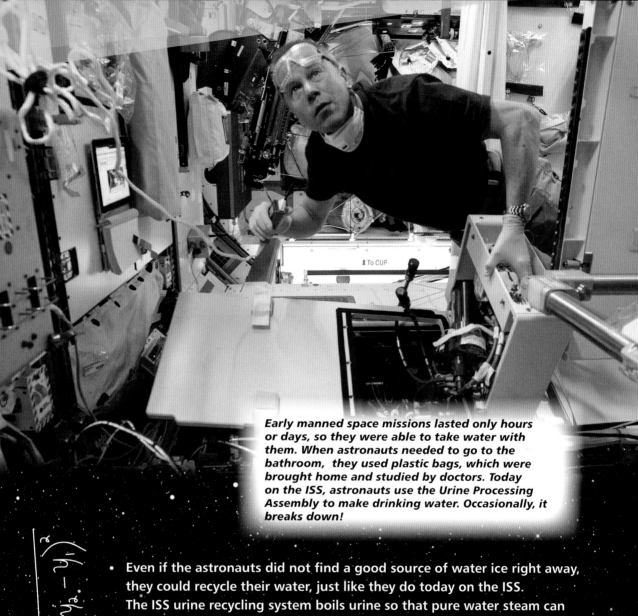

Early manned space missions lasted only hours or days, so they were able to take water with them. When astronauts needed to go to the bathroom, they used plastic bags, which were brought home and studied by doctors. Today on the ISS, astronauts use the Urine Processing Assembly to make drinking water. Occasionally, it breaks down!

Even if the astronauts did not find a good source of water ice right away, they could recycle their water, just like they do today on the ISS. The ISS urine recycling system boils urine so that pure water steam can be collected, condensed (turned from gas to a liquid), and drunk safely.

Practice Makes Perfect

Like everything else in space exploration, it is good to practice living in Mars's conditions on Earth first. The HI-SEAS base is a pretend Mars base on the slopes of Hawaii's Mauna Loa volcano. Six "astronauts" live and work there for up to a year while being watched by scientists and doctors. They are studying the effect of isolation from Earth. Not being able to make calls to family could cause loneliness and stress, which could endanger the mission.

$d = \sqrt{(x_2 - x_1) + (y_2 - y_1)^2}$

BUILDING ON MARS

Getting into space is expensive. Mars missions will cost even more than the space shuttle and ISS. Every piece of equipment we send to Mars means a bigger rocket and more fuel. SpaceX believes the mission would cost around $3,000 per pound of equipment, but it is likely to cost much more. Anything you could make on Mars would make the mission more affordable.

3-D Printing

Printing solid objects in **three dimensions (3-D)** has been around since the 1980s. In recent years, technological leaps have made it popular. A 3-D computer **simulation** of an object is used; the printer then makes the object by printing tiny layers on top of each other. Instead of printer ink, the printer uses fine powder that can be metallic or plastic. As the powder builds up each layer, a laser can be used to melt it and fuse it to the rest of the layers below. Cars, airplane parts, and whole houses have been made with 3-D printing.

3-D printers can make almost any shape. This one has made a spool holder.

Printing in Space

The Zero-G Printer was sent to the ISS in 2014 via a SpaceX cargo ship. NASA then emailed a 3-D computer model of a socket wrench to the station. The astronauts printed this. Tools like socket wrenches are often lost during spacewalks, so the ability to replace simple objects in space is an important milestone. Another project is experimenting with printing parts for a base on the moon, using artificial lunar soil.

Be a Space Scientist!

Imagine that you have a 3-D printer on Mars. What would you build? Which objects would be better to build there than to bring from Earth? How would we know in advance what could actually be made from Mars rocks and soil?

$$d = \sqrt{(x_2 - x_1) + (y_2 - y_1)^2}$$

US astronaut Barry Wilmore worked with the 3-D printer sent to the ISS in 2014. The socket wrench made on board is a simple hand tool, but it proved that the ISS could make spare parts in orbit. The blueprint was beamed from Earth by radio directly to the printer.

41

$$d = \sqrt{(x_2 - x_1) + (y_2 - y_1)^2}$$

MARS BECOMES EARTH

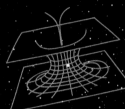

Scientists believe that billions of years ago, Mars was much more like Earth than it is today, so it would be the easiest planet to change. Turning Mars into Earth would be the greatest engineering project of all time.

What to Change?

To make Mars more like Earth, three things would need to change: the thickness of the atmosphere, the temperature, and protection against **radiation** from the Sun. Remember, the air on Mars is only one-hundredth as thick as Earth's. If you stood on Mars without a spacesuit, the saliva on your tongue and the tears in your eyes would instantly boil off. The same would also happen to the water in your lungs, resulting in a quick and very unpleasant death!

Melting the polar caps would make water and carbon dioxide. As the planet became more like Earth, plant life would begin to flourish, and oceans would fill the low points of the surface.

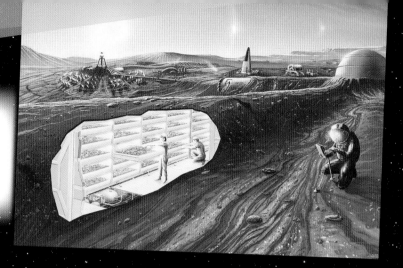

Here, you can see many of parts of a Mars base. In the distance is the rocket to bring people home. Underground in the foreground is a greenhouse for growing plants.

Moon Dust

One idea would be to sprinkle dark dust from Mars' two small moons, Phobos and Deimos, onto the bright polar caps. These icy regions would then absorb heat from the sun instead of reflecting it. This would also make the caps start to melt, which would release large amounts of carbon dioxide and water vapor into the air. Like on Earth, carbon dioxide would be a **greenhouse gas**, which traps heat from the sun in the atmosphere. Frozen ices from the outer solar system could be added to the air to make it thicker and warmer.

Once you had raised the temperature and thickened the air enough, you could start planting simple plant life, such as lichens and mosses, which would start changing carbon dioxide into oxygen. You could then make an ozone layer from oxygen, which would shield the surface from the sun's harmful rays, like it does on Earth. After perhaps hundreds of years, people would be able to walk on Mars with the same kind of suit and oxygen supply used by mountaineers on Earth.

BE A SPACE SCIENTIST! ANSWERS

Pages 8–9 Why Colonize Mars?

1. Venus is almost the same size and **mass** as Earth, and so it has almost the same gravity. The high temperatures and pressures there mean you would need a very heavy and bulky suit to survive.
2. Mars has the most similar temperature range to Earth and almost the same length of day.
3. The Martian temperature and length of day would make it easier for humans to adjust to than the other planets.

Pages 14–15 Getting Dressed for Space

A spacesuit made for use on Mars would need to be lighter than the ones used on the moon. This is because the gravity is greater on Mars.

Pages 20–21 Choosing Where to Land

Martian dust would be a problem for astronauts. Martian dust storms, like the one *Mariner 9* found in 1971, can cover the entire planet. Dust storms on Mars can last months and would affect communications and solar power, as well as clogging up equipment.

Pages 26–27 Setting up Base

It would be best to land in a low level on the map rather than in mountainous places. The blue areas on the map show low levels. Areas near the equator are warmer than areas farther away from it. Therefore, a spot in the blue area on the map and near the equator would be a good place to land.

Pages 32–33 Choose Your Crew

You would need people who are excellent pilots, a doctor, and an engineer who can fix things that go wrong. An expert in geology, such as the one on *Apollo 17*, would be useful when exploring the planet. A weather expert was not needed to explore the moon, since it has no air. But on Mars, the weather causes dust storms, so a specialist would be helpful.

Pages 40–41 Building on Mars

You would bring small, lightweight objects such as computer processors from Earth. Anything big and heavy would need to be made on Mars. You could make construction materials — "Mars bricks," for example — using 3-D printers. We know what the Martian soil and rocks are made from because of the samples taken by landers and rovers.

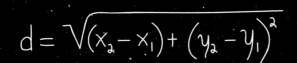

$$d = \sqrt{(x_2 - x_1) + (y_2 - y_1)^2}$$

GLOSSARY

adapted When the features of an organism's body, or of its behavior, have changed to help it survive.

altitude Height above sea level.

asteroid Large rock found in the solar system.

atmosphere Thin blanket of gas surrounding a planet.

chemistry The study of what matter is made of and how it changes.

civilizations Complex societies of people who have developed communities, and culture, including writing or other types of communication.

climate The usual pattern of weather that happens in a place.

climate change Changes in the world's weather patterns caused by human activity.

Cold War A period of great tension between the United States and the USSR in the second half of the twentieth century.

colonize To take over an area to control it and live in it.

comet A space object that has a long, bright tail when it passes near the Sun.

cosmonaut A Russian astronaut.

environment The natural world in which plants and animals live.

evolved Gradually changed over time.

extinction When all the members of a single species have died out.

fertilizers Anything added to soil to improve the growth of plants.

friction The force that slows down an object when it is moving against another object or material.

geology The study of rocks and the surface and interior of Earth.

gravity The pull that any object has on any other. The bigger the object or planet, the more gravity it has.

greenhouse gas A gas that traps heat in the atmosphere.

heat shield An almost flat, tough surface on a spacecraft that absorbs the heat of an entry into a planet's atmosphere.

infrared Invisible light emitted by heated objects.

landers Space probes that can land on a planet or moon and take measurements.

mass The total amount of matter that an object has, measured in weight.

mass extinction Short periods in Earth's history when lots of species have died out for the same reasons.

microbes Tiny life forms, including germs, that can be seen only with a microscope.

minerals Substances in nature that do not come from living things.

missiles Self-propelling airborne or space-borne vehicles. A space rocket is a type of missile.

mission control The people who control a space mission on Earth, and the place in which they work.

nuclear bomb A device that uses nuclear reactions to explode.

nuclear disasters Human-made catastrophes that could happen during a war using nuclear weapons.

optical illusion Something that happens when the eyes are tricked into seeing something that is not there.

orbit The circular or oval path one object follows around another in space, due to the pull of its gravity.

organisms Living things.

overpopulation When there are too many members of a species for the amount of food and other resources it needs.

polar caps Regions around a planet's north and south poles where ice has formed.

pressurized Filled with air or other gas.

$$d = \sqrt{(x_2 - x_1)^2 + (y_2 - y_1)^2}$$

probes Unmanned spacecraft designed for exploration.

radiation Energy in the form of waves or rays that cannot be seen.

retro-rockets Rocket engines designed to slow down a spacecraft.

robotic Capable of carrying out simple instructions without human intervention.

rovers Wheeled vehicles used to explore other planets.

satellite An object in space that can be natural, such as a planet's moon, or artificial, such as a communication satellite.

simulation Something that imitates how something will work in real life.

solar nebula A vast cloud of gas and dust in space that collapsed under its own gravity to form the solar system.

solar system The Sun, its planets and moons, asteroids, and comets.

Space Age The time in history when space exploration became possible.

space station An outpost in space that stays in the same place and acts as a laboratory.

space tourism Traveling into space for fun and to see what is there.

species A type of animal or plant.

sterile Not able to produce growing things, such as crops or plants.

telescope A tubelike instrument that lets a person view objects in space by making them look bigger.

tether A flexible line or tube connecting an astronaut to a spacecraft during a spacewalk.

three dimensions (3-D) Length, width, and height of an object.

topographic maps Maps that show the height and depth of features on a planet's surface.

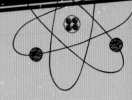

FURTHER READING

BOOKS

Aldrin, Buzz and Marianne Dyson. *Welcome to Mars: Making a Home on the Red Planet*. Washington, D.C.: National Geographic Kids, 2015.

Carney, Elizabeth. *Mars: The Red Planet: Rocks, Rovers, Pioneers, and More!* Washington, D.C.: National Geographic Kids, 2016.

Carney, Elizabeth. *Mars* (National Geographic Readers). Washington, D.C.: National Geographic Kids, 2014.

Lee, Pascal. *Mission: Mars*. New York, NY: Scholastic, 2013.

Rusch, Elizabeth. *The Mighty Mars Rovers: The Incredible Adventures of Spirit and Opportunity* (Scientists in the Field). Boston, MA: HMH Books for Young Readers, 2012.

WEBSITES

Due to the changing nature of Internet links, PowerKids Press has developed an online list of websites related to the subject of this book. This site is updated regularly. Please use this link to access the list: **www.powerkidslinks.com/bass/mars**

INDEX